TREMBLING HEART

KATHARINE STONE AYERS

First Edition September 2015
Second Edition October 2016

Flowing Rivers Publications

ISBN-13: 978-0-9965968-4-8

ISBN-10: 099659844

Enjoy Katharine's art at: www.katharinestoneayers.com

Cover and book design by Cherri LaMarr

Other Books by Katharine Stone Ayers

Old Remnants New Buds

Opening

From Frozenness to Freedom

Dedication

to Love

Dear Poetry Lovers and Friends,

As human beings we all know the gifts and challenges of relationships, whether with other human beings, oneself, plants, animals, nature or Essence. Some say that relationships can be our greatest challenge and our greatest gift, including an opportunity for transformation. I've certainly experienced both challenges and gifts: from dissention, frustration, and betrayal to satisfaction, bliss and intimate connection.

These poems chronicle my experiences with relationships, from first loves to pets, nature and eventually more conscious and intimate relationships with friends, partners, Presence and myself.

I know what it's like to be in the throes of historical dramas, traumas, old worn out behaviors, projections and distorted views of reality. I also know that it's possible to experience a whole new level of intimacy with others and myself. How does this happen? By being able to let veils, illusions, obscurations, old habits and conditioning drop. This takes awareness, being present and accepting moment-to-moment experience as it arises. It also takes openness, vulnerability, curiosity, surrender and true courage – concepts that are not always popular with ego mind.

As I explore, understand and see how I've been conditioned by my history, culture, societal values, the media, I can make new choices, open to new behaviors and healthier perspectives. My view of life can change in a way the is fresh and supportive. When I notice the projections and overlays I have on others and reality, the capacity to see and love another becomes more possible. Clarity, peace, love, vulnerability, compassion, strength and other aspects of Presence can arise spontaneously.

To experience the alchemy of relationship means I can gradually learn tolerate and embrace my moment to moment experience, such as deep longing, despair, hopelessness, helplessness, rage, hatred, anger, joy beauty, peace, compassion. By learning to allow and not censor what flows through my consciousness, life gets richer. I become more capable of real relating on a deeper and more satisfying level. Personal love takes on a quality that becomes more universal. I can become more peaceful, settled and accepting what is.

I want to thank my poetry mentor, Lorraine Mejia, who has helped me organize these poems into a volume, given me quality feedback and inspired guidance on revising and enriching my poetry. Thanks to Cherri LaMarr, who has done an artful job of book design and given me excellent feedback on the actual creation of my book. A special thanks to my friends who have cheered me on.

My wish is that these poems will resonate with some of your experiences and support you in allowing deeper compassion, love and understanding of yourself and others.

17   Because the Heart

CASCADE OF STARS

21   Hand of Destiny

23   Cascade of Stars

25   Connection

27   Simply Being

29   First Love

31   The Note

33   Bigger Than Life

35   Longing

37   Blessing

39   The First Thirty Years of My Life

41   For John

43   The Embrace

45   Together

47   True Love

49   Learning to Love

51   Love

VEILS

55   Let Love Flow Again

57   Do I Dare

59   Do We Know Each Other?

61   Being

63   Heart's Journey

65   Narcissus

67 Just Because

69 Don't Bludgeon Me

71 Shall I, Because You...

73 You Who Inspire

75 Veil

77 Limits and Trust

79 How I Like Me

83 If Your Arms

SCENT OF JASMINE

87 Benie, You And I...

89 Benie And I

91 Azure Blue

95 Scent of Jasmine for Benie

101 Rosie

103 Ohia Forest

105 My Dog Runs

107 Hurricane Warning

109 Cadinals

111 Mynah Bird

113 Rosie Snores

115 Moment

117 Love

PRESENCE DANCES
in the SPACE between us

121   The Space Between Them

123   Our Words Like Gems

125   Touched by Georgia

127   Deborah

131   For JONIA

133   My Cup Runneth Over...

135   Healing

137   Alchemy

139   The Circle is Complete

143   Beauty Emerges

LET LOVE FLOW

147   O Brother Sister

149   Fun

153   Silent Longing

155   Memories That Heal

157   Let Love Flow

159   Miracles

161   I Know

163   Impermanence

165   Trembling heart

Footprints in the Sand photo by Katharine Stone Ayers

BECAUSE the HEART

Because the terns protect their young, the ocean
Because the sun warms the sand beneath my feet, the fire
Because today I pot black purple orchids, the earth
Because the clouds were swept away last night, the wind
Because a vast luminous space opens, the Heart

CASCADE OF STARS

HAND of DESTINY

brought you to me,
me to you.

Blessed connection!

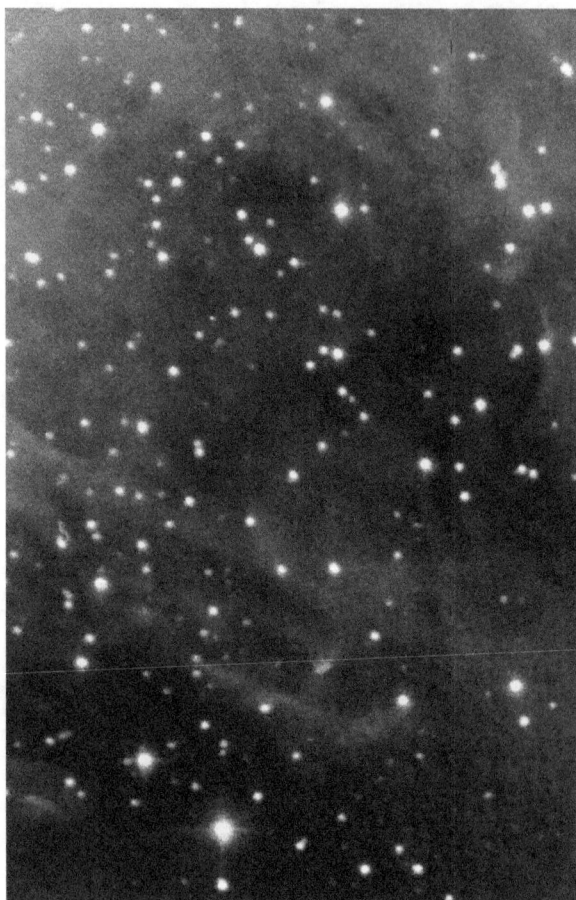

CASCADE of STARS

What constellates
my life
into
a cascade of stars?

something magical, greater
than anything that I can dream up
with my ordinary mind.

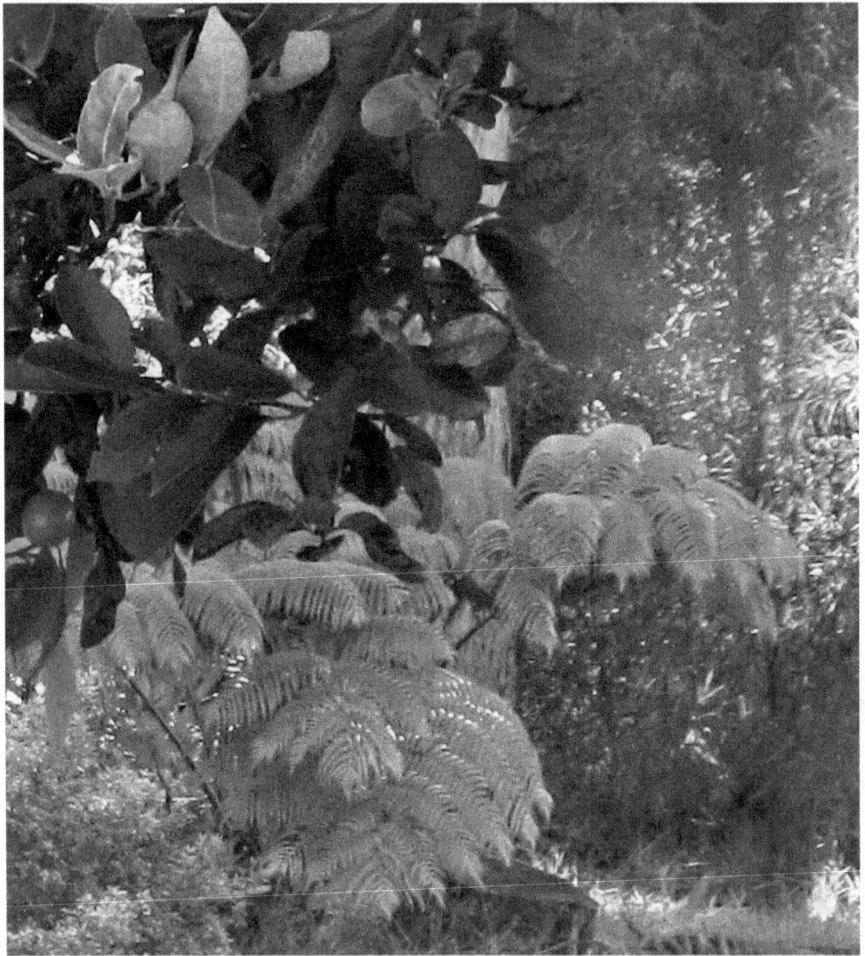

Leafy Green photo by Katharine Stone Ayers

CONNECTION

You ask me,
"What's right about holding onto your conviction in your individual self?"

"Of course I'm me.
Who else would I be?
What else could I turn into?
Where would I go?
And if I went somewhere
what would happen to me?"

I, me, mine
pervades everything **I** do
I wash the dishes, **I** pick roses, **I** take a bath.
I sing, **I** dance, **I** write
You talk to me.
This chair is **mine**. So is this book.
That's just the way it is.

I keep answering the question.
A vast spaciousness opens in my head.

The question becomes irrelevant.

Leafy green growth fountains in my chest.
My heart opens softly.
We relate to each other
delicate, luminous, precious.

All parts of me relax, basque
in a gentle exquisitely attuned Presence —
every cell massaged into infinity.

Here we are together.
innocent young smiling eyes
and faces.

SIMPLY BEING

Here we are
I see you
you see me

we are
totally present
to one another

simply being
ordinary and extraordinary
vast and particular
nothing excluded
everything included
warts, fingers, toes, wrinkles
your worries and concerns
my fears
racing thoughts
aching bodies

simple grace
gentle compassion
deep love

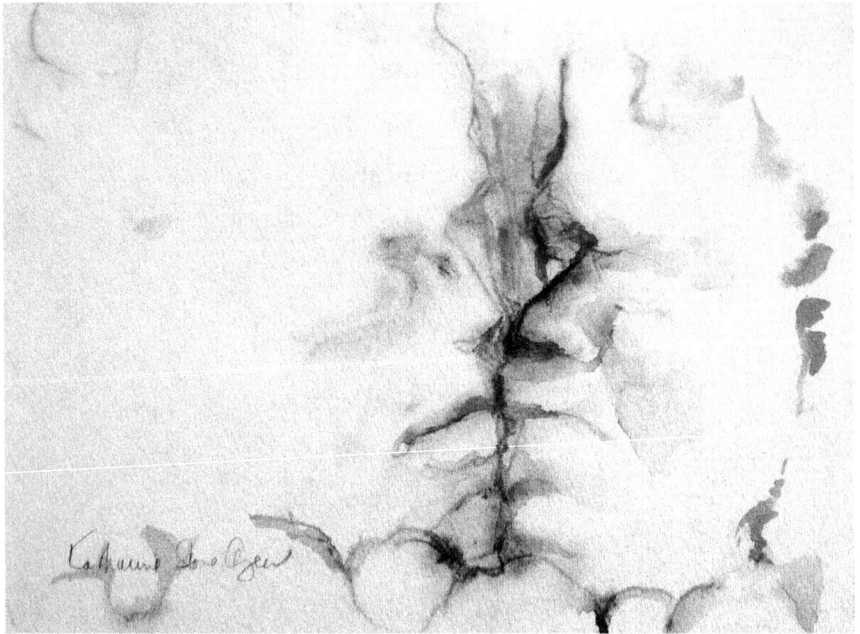

Kissing Pots watercolor by Katharine Stone Ayers

FIRST LOVE

You were the best kisser.
Your full lips against mine
exploring dozens of ways to kiss.

Your long black eyelashes
hovered over your deep dark eyes
mesmerized me into silent longing.

I yielded to your soft young body
you to mine.

In the cushy front seat of your shiny maroon car
(that you waxed and polished that day)
I leaned into you,
let myself disappear into
timelessness.

THE NOTE

I remember how
my heart thumped loudly
when I wrote
you a note
with a dark pencil
on blue lined paper
folded it into a little square
stuck it
in your pocket

how my heart
melted
when you opened it
looked coyly
at me
sunshine smiles
emanating from your precious face

BIGGER THAN LIFE

You gave me your hand
when I was lost
in a stinking hell hole
swirling downwards
into murky mud green waters.

powerless,
I kept sinking,
couldn't find
safety or light.

Your compassionate blue eyes,
your care, kindness
coaxed me out

into sunshine
joy, pleasure, sensuality
aliveness

You were bigger than life.

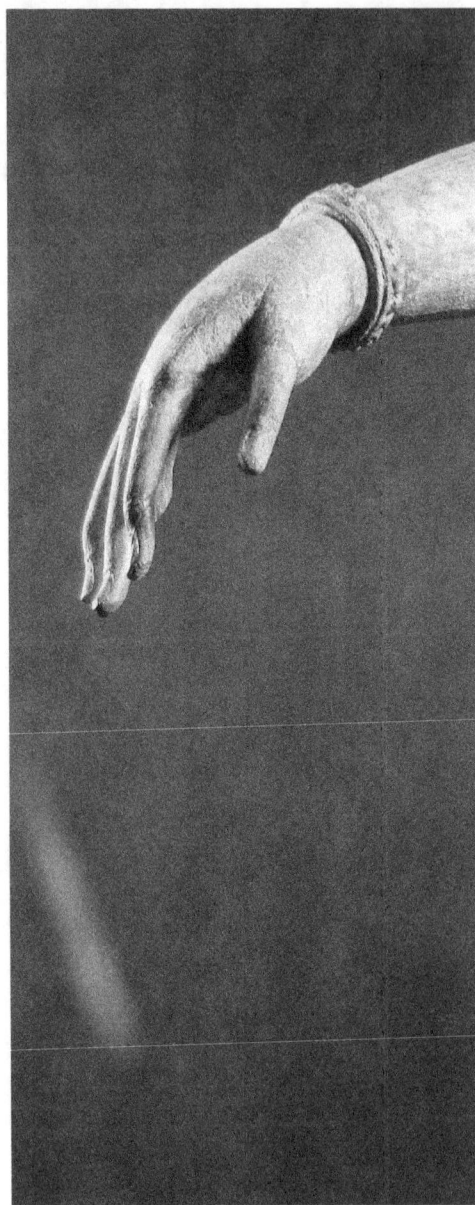

Hand with Rainbow
photo by Katharine Stone Ayers

LONGING

I wanna touch you
all over.

I want to touch
your neck
your face
your eyes!

My fingers want to explore the depth
of
who you are.

I *wanna* touch you.

Great longing in my heart.
every cell longing!

Who is this you I want to touch?

Delicacy and tenderness
notes of resonance
dance between us.

I want to celebrate the
preciousness that flows
between us,

remember not to displace
longing, delicacy and tenderness
outside myself, but

let it nourish, morph, grow
inside me.

BLESSING

In this soft and
expansive place

I see you
you see me.

We are held by the Universe.

You help me navigate through
rough waters.
You look at me with awe,
encouragement,
love
in your heart.

I connect with my
True Self.

Door acrylic painting by Katharine Stone Ayers

The FIRST THIRTY YEARS OF MY LIFE

I prided myself in not needing anyone.

I told myself
"I don't need you."
"It's okay if you leave."
"It doesn't bother me."

You taught me
about love.
Veneers and rigidities
began to melt.

A door in my heart opened.

FOR JOHN

I knocked.
You opened a door.

I stepped into
a realm of luminosity,
tenderness, delicacy,
loveliness.

Embrace drawing by Katharine Stone Ayers

THE EMBRACE

You hug me,
hold me close and tight
against the length
of your body.

I stop breathing.
(You've taken me by surprise!)

My breasts melt into your chest
I relax
breathe into the sweetness of the moment,
delicate rivulets of sensuality
circulate and flow everywhere.

You touch my face ever so tenderly
I'm transported into another realm.
You stroke my hair ever so softly.
A gentle light moves through me

I hold you tightly, stroke your back,
want to know you more deeply.

Precious moment of blessed intimacy

lingers on
like a lullaby.

Poppy photo by Katharine Stone Ayers

TOGETHER

Together
goodness
strength

Together
song and music
longing, weeping and joy
bowing before the infinite.

Together
dancing
unfolding
a poem, a rose, a flower.

Whispering together
in the dawn
in the evening.
remembering and forgetting
together

Together
a bond
unity
building
stretching, expanding
opening
spinning

Leaving space
to grow and transform
together
and separately

Loving
growing together
painting, writing,
playing
together.

TRUE LOVE

Is it normal?
No, it's natural.

I thought I found true love.
When it was gone,
I wondered,
Did I make it up?
Was it a fantasy?"

When an excommunicated Catholic priest turned psychic
told me at our wedding reception
that we had many lifetimes together,
said we'd come together this time
to complete our journey,
tears came to my eyes.

I assumed that we would live happily ever after.

I forgot to notice
all the lifetimes
that we took turns betraying each other,

Bliss turned into bickering,
we tried to salvage our relationship,
did therapy, went to seminars
took communications courses,
went to Marriage encounter.

But in the end
unresolved traumas blew us apart.

After we separated, I told him,
"You're treating me like I don't exist."

He said, *"You don't.*

I told myself, "Never again.
Relationships are too difficult."

Then you walked into my life,
stood next to me.
Waves of joy and bliss moved through me,
My cynical philosophy
evaporated.

You shook my foundation.

LEARNING TO LOVE

I'm doing it differently this time.
I'm not compromising, accommodating
or rushing to take care of your needs.

I take care of me and my needs,
have learned to focus on
what makes me happy,
allows my soul to sing and dance.

I take risks
that bring up doubt and shame,
embarrass myself
by being uncompromisingly real,
leave space for your no's,
you honor mine.

I notice
how supportive, kind
deep, thoughtful and sensitive you are,
how you appreciate and encourage me.

I ask myself,
Can I begin again?

Katharine S. Ogus

LOVE

opens my eyes,
strips me naked.

VEILS

Veil of Old Patterns photo by Chelsea

LET LOVE FLOW AGAIN

When I was young,
I wanted to serve others,
I thought this was how to express love.

I was shocked to discover
how I stopped love from flowing
by being
overly focused
on helping others,
not loving myself,
getting wounded,
holding resentment,
being self critical.

"Time out!"

Leave the old patterns behind.
let love flow again.

Red Roses photo by Katharine Stone Ayers

DO I DARE

Do I dare
Do I dare to
Do I dare to imagine

that my heart will open
love deeply again?

DO WE KNOW EACH OTHER?

I think I know you.
You think you know me.

How much of our ideas,
perspectives, beliefs
about each other
are an illusion?

BEING

Veils drop from my eyes

I see you
simply
without frills

not
trying to impress you,
please you,
worry about how I'm doing

My mind
isn't chattering about the past
how things should be done
or the future
hoping that the pain will get better

I'm simply here
quietly allowing joy
to bubble up

Joy and Freedom painting by Katharine Stone Ayers

HEART'S JOURNEY

I thought you liked me
for having the courage
to be who I am.

I stopped editing and censoring
myself.

I practiced being real and authentic
with my thoughts, feelings, aspirations,
said what was meaningful
important to me, wrote you poetry,
spoke from my soul.

My heart opened to new freedom and joy.

I thought you were practicing being real too.

You started to withdraw, didn't say what was going on.

I mourned
not having the chance
to know you more deeply.

Heartbreak played havoc with me for a while.

but didn't stop me
from continuing to be myself,

embrace joy and freedom.

NARCISSUS

Your shining star shape
white perfume
seduces me.

Do I freeze
in astonishment
looking at my reflection?

Is it narcissistic
to take care
of my needs?

JUST BECAUSE

Just because you shut me out of your heart
doesn't mean that I shut the door to my heart.

> I can hold grief and hurt around my heart
> in compassion,
> experience barriers dissolve,
> celebrate being home again.

DON'T BLUDGEON ME

with harsh words,
force your version of reality on me,

It could be different for me.

Let me have
my experience,
honor
my timing,
my rhythm,
in my unique way.

I can follow my thread.

Our threads, yours and mine,
are woven,
of something Divine,

intertwined.

SHALL I, BECAUSE YOU...

Shall I bury my affection
because you don't respond to me?

Shall I let my poetry
love
aliveness
passion
fade,
because you're not available.

Shall I stop writing
or wanting you?

Shall I wrap my heart up in soft cloth
and bind it with twine,
because your aren't open?

Shall I react the way I did with Dad,
pout and say "I don't care",
because I fear the pain
of being shamed, humiliated.

Why should I continue
to dampen my aliveness when I remember
how he turned away,
left over and over again?

I remind myself
that it is okay
to feel pain, hurt, rage,
accept the freeze
that happens under extreme duress,
honor the elegant way my body
learned to protect itself.

As the freeze melts,
I pray I can gently sense myself,
thoughtfully allow
what arises as a gift

move on
to a brighter life.

YOU WHO INSPIRE

When I am around someone who loves and is patient,
I learn to be loving and patient.
When someone is hateful and impatient
I learn what not to do.
When you take precious care of yourself,
I get inspired to do that too.
When you are kind and good hearted,
my heart starts to sing.

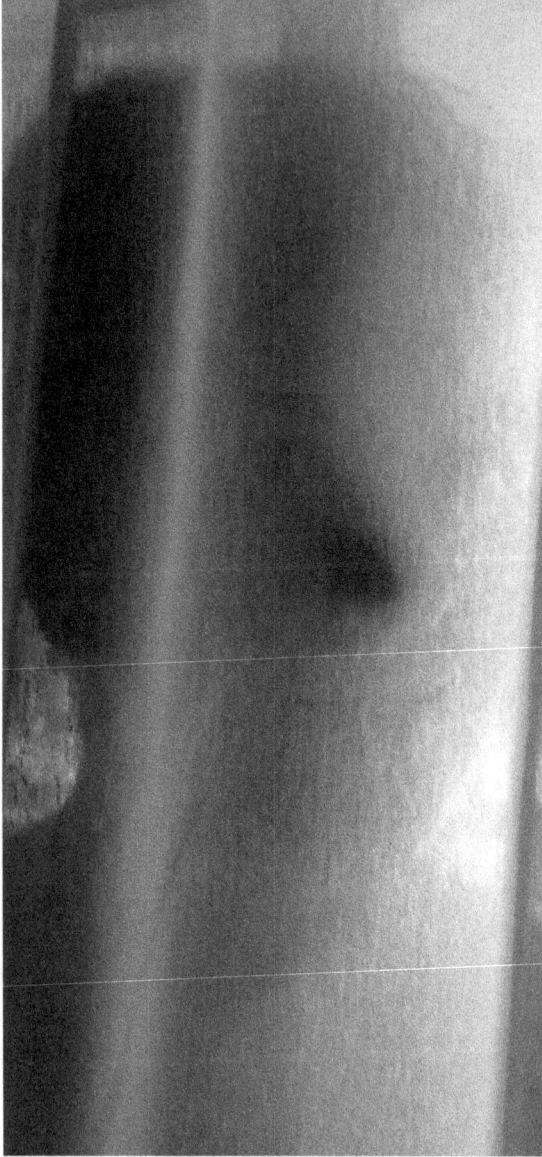

Veil photo by Katharine Stone Ayers

VEIL

As I look at you,
I'm surprised to discover that I see you
through a veil.

I get a subtle whiff
of a pattern formed in my consciousness
a long time ago.

(A sense of being a little kid
who peers out at out at you cautiously.
She's shy,
embarrassed
not sure of herself,
afraid of being criticized, blamed,
put down, diminished, made to feel small,
humiliated.)

When I see this veil,
(understand
that I am not this wounded child)
it lifts magically,
dissolves.

In this moment I no longer
struggle or push myself
to be with you.

Barriers melt.
An ease flows in the space between us.

LIMITS AND TRUST

Limits
a word that resonates
in my heart.
Permission to have limits-
the safety and comfort
that limits provide.

Relaxation moves through my chest
and whole body
as I take in the word:
Limits.

You say the word
"Trust."

How beautiful to trust you
knowing you speak the truth.

I can trust me
to have the strength to be real,
the power to change,
courage to communicate honestly,

care for myself deeply,
step away from playing power games
of one-up, one down.

come back to sanity, wholeness
know
what rings true.

HOW I LIKE ME

When I was weak and vapid,
this is how you liked me.

When I was quiet, shy and demure,
this is how you liked me.

If I didn't assert myself or have opinions,
this is how you liked me.

As long as I agreed with you,
this is how you liked me.

As long as I laughed at your sick, off color jokes,
this is how you liked me.

When I gave you my adulation,
knocked myself out to please you,
this is how you liked me.

As long as I didn't have needs,
this is how you liked me.

That was then.

Now this is how I like me:

Strong

Vital

Speaking out

Saying what's real

Embracing my needs

Centered

Grounded

True to myself

Loving what's beautiful and natural

Nurturing myself

with caring friends

attuned lovers

wholesome plants, animals,

clean food, air and water.

Speaking the Truth.

This is how I like me.

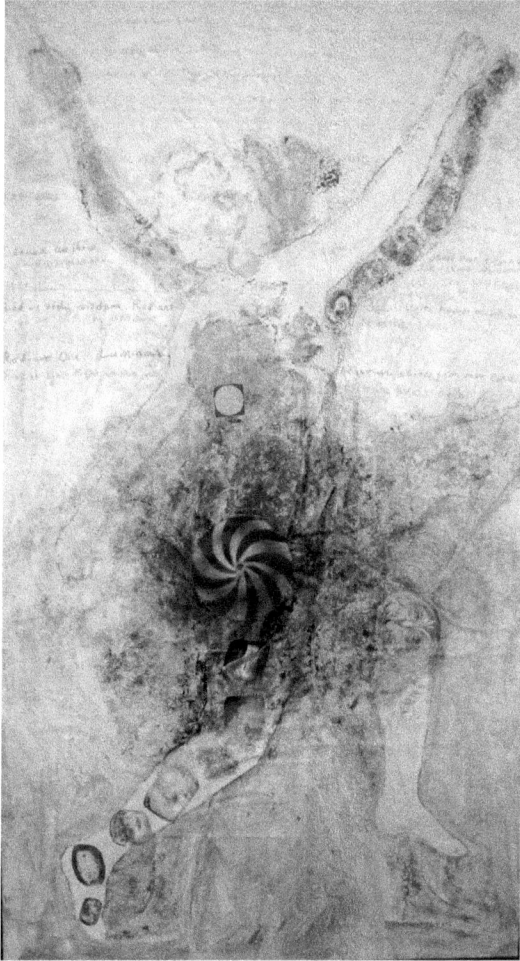

Empowered Acrylic by Katharine Stone Ayers

Bamboo photo by Katharine Stone Ayers

IF YOUR ARMS

If I linger in your arms a little longer
let your kisses embrace me in a spiral of sparkles.

If the birth of this day could release my longing.

If I could let the morning sun
on the green of bamboo leaves and eucalyptus
trickle through my heart.

If I could express how deeply
your kindness runs like a river
through my bones.

If the bees suck all the nectar
from the blue borage flowers today
and build another honeycomb in their little white house.

If your soul song moves joyfully
through me.

If you gather up all my grief
into your beautiful, capable, attuned hands—
toss it into blue infinity.

SCENT OF JASMINE

Benie photo by Katharine Stone Ayers

BENIE, YOU AND I...

we love contact.

My feet on your spine.
You push your back into the soles of my feet.

I lie on my back.
take in earth,
clouds
feel your belly breathing.

I'm filled up, alive

connected to myself,
to you.
ocean,
wind,
my body.

full of earth energy,
sea, sky, dog.

Refreshed

I surrender to the
softness of
this moment.

Benie photo by Katharine Stone Ayers

BENIE AND I

Benie
My feet on your bum.
My legs against your belly.

You're
taking a nap,
catching flies.

Me being me.

When I withdraw my energy,
forget that I
am still
connected with you,
your questioning eyes look.

Benie photo by Katharine Stone Ayers

AZURE BLUE

I ask for a dream about my life and health,
and dream a disturbing dream.

Benie in an azure blue swimming pool
barely able to doggie paddle.
Weak.

He's a Golden Retriever. He loves the water. He'll be okay.

But in my heart, I'm concerned and wonder
if he can swim strongly enough to hold his head above the
water...

I see him again.
weaker now...barely paddling.
I'm terrified that he is going to drown.
He's inhaling water.

I jump in the water, swim to him
press my body against his back,
wrap my arms around his chest,
interlace my fingers around his heart.

I'm relieved that his heart is still beating.
I kick to push him to safety.

Benie, please don't die!
Please don't die, Benie!
Help! Help! Somebody help me to help Benie!

I wake up.
uncomfortable, distressed

My precious dog who wants to please everyone
My animal companion who is so exuberant and transparent,
who mopes when I am sad.
wants affection and closeness,
insists on dislodging my pen with his nose
when I pay bills to remind me
what's important.

Why are you dying Benie?
I don't want you to die.

I'm immersed in an ocean of blue stillness.
Oh! I'm in Benie's pool!
Water is enveloping me.
I want to keep swimming.
I can't.
It's too much effort.

I smell fragrant flowers, Benie,
like the morning you died.

Scent of jasmine floating on the air.
the scent of you, dear Benie,
your Presence lingering on

Benie
Bene
Benediction

Benie photo by Katharine Stone Ayers

SCENT OF JASMINE
for Benie

I watch fire consume the flesh around your face. Flames melt your lips. You look like you are barring your teeth. That's not like you. I don't remember a time when you snarled. You were always smiling. Men and women, children and babies...you went up to them all, wagging your tail with gentle enthusiasm. Even when they shooed you away, you moved on happily to greet another. When we walked along the lava ocean cliffs, I watched while you waded in tide pools, dunking your head in the water, trying to catch fish. You never caught any, but that didn't faze you.

The flames continue to engulf the flesh of your head. Your soft parts disappear. Only your bones remain.

A golden harmony, equanimity and peace pervade the air. The fire is fiercely hot, so I position myself on a rock at the periphery of the stone circle to move away from the searing heat. Your body has been burning quietly in the center of the circle for many hours.

———————•◆•———————

Four days before you die, I have a dream.

I dream that my friend, Beverly, and I are going to La Bourgogne, our favorite French restaurant. Benie is in the car with us. Bev leans down to pet him and is startled when she sees blood on her hand. Benie is bleeding from his penis, which is bloody and soggy. As I look down, I see there is a hole in the bottom of his pelvis that looks like a sink bowl with blood fountaining up and filling the basin.

He's bleeding to death. I hold him. His face turns grey with white speckles. He gets older and older and older. He's dying. I tell him how much I love him and how special he is. He says, *Do you know I love you?* Real affection moves silently between us.

———◆———

I watch you, Benie, when I get up each morning, as you lie contentedly on the mat next to the kitchen doorstep. Your eyes look like they are in another world. Sometimes your head shakes and you have difficulty getting up. I try to coax you to come for a walk. You're too exhausted. I want you to eat and drink. I drip a few drops of water into your mouth from a turkey baster, but you turn your head away. I worry. I try homeopathic remedies, prayer, talking to you. I don't want to believe that it is time for you to go.

Needing a break from my worry and concern about you, I drive up the mountain to spend the night at Beverly's. The next morning I wake up feeling uneasy.

I feel a strong pull to go home.

When I get to my driveway, I'm horrified to see you lying at the edge of the garage. You are practically motionless and only a few inches from a pile of poop. You're covered with black flies, unable to move. Angrily I shoo the flies away, *"Get away! Get away! He's not dead yet!"* The flies keep coming back.

Sobbing I call the vet. "Clean him up and spray some fly repellent on him. He's got lymphatic sarcoma. It's spread and there is nothing I can do."

I bathe you, spray Buzz Away citronella on your fur and cover you with towels. As I watch you and your labored breathing, the day seems incredibly long. I light some large white candles. I decide to spend the day with you while I sort and clean stuff out of the garage. I just want to be near you. I pray that you are comfortable.

I call my friend Barbara and tell her that you have stopped drinking, "He's dying, Kitty. I stayed with my cat when she was dying, and that's how it is. They stop eating and drinking." I cry for a long time.

I light some incense and sort through more stuff. Once and awhile I try to give you a little water. You move your head away again, even though your throat makes reflexive swallowing movements.

The next day a friend comes to help me. We roll you onto a sheet and carry you in a sling to a shady place under the plumeria tree while we do chores in the kitchen. I hose you off, return to the chores, positioning myself so I can see you through the kitchen window.

You lie practically motionless for most of the day. I feel helpless as I watch you follow me with your eyes. If only there was something I could do. The wind comes up, so we prepare to move you to a safe spot in the garage where you will be protected. We turn you over. My friend gasps. Weeping open sores are all over the side of your body. They aren't healing. Your hair is matted. You can no longer lift your head. Your body sags like a rag doll as we lift you on to a sheet and carry you to your resting place in the garage.

Beverly calls, "I'm concerned. Hadn't we better put him down?"

My heart sinks at her suggestion. I say, "I want to be with him until he leaves on his own. I don't think he'll last the night."

"Then I'm going to come over."

I wake up around three o'clock. I feel very lightheaded. The air seems rarefied. I sense a luminous Presence. The space fills with golden light…

Bev awakens. We hold hands and walk to the garage together.

You take long deep breaths with very long exhales. *"You really are dying,"* I say quietly to myself.

> *Are Benie's long exhales his way*
> *of breathing himself out of his body?*

I look down at you for a long time. I wish really hard that I will see your chest continue to move, but it is utterly still. I look at you in awe…you breathed yourself effortlessly into another realm.

My tears fall softly on the cement floor of the garage. I feel relief for your graceful passing.

I stroke your body and I hold your paw one last time. Beverly and I cover you with a blanket. We hug each other.

I smell the scent of jasmine.

Later that morning we put your body in the back of my car and take you to Barbara's home at Paleaku Gardens. We walk toward a circle that is orientated to the four directions. There is an ascension stone in the middle. A Native American built and dedicated this sacred circle for the cremation of our animal friends.

We place you on a large koa plank, adorn your body with flowers and incense. Barbara places a kata around your eyes. We build a fire. I light it.

The air is pervaded with utter peace and harmony.

So like you Benie…peace, joy and equanimity.

Rosie photo by Pam

ROSIE

Rosie who shadows me everywhere
wants to be close
who says she loves me more than anything
who asks what she can do to heal me
is clear about what she wants
takes the salmon snack bag out of the closet
drops it at my feet.
licks lillikoi and macademia nut butter from my fingers
leans her silky fur and waxy ear canal into my hand
whose fur is black, soft, shiny
who has cakes of red dirt on her nose from burying bones
rolls in red dirt until she turns into a chocolate lab
who sleeps while I meditate
who barks to get in
barks to get out
who sniffed raw fish this morning
waited until the hornets left
chomped fiercely on fish skin with her back teeth
had bad breath
who is cautious, sometimes submissive
snaps at yappy little dogs and big dogs who sniff her butt
who never learned how to play, chase balls or sit up
is happy to stay, lie down or heel if she wants to
who is older now
farts, breathes heavily, snores loudly at my bedside
grey hairs on her chin and paws
is sunshine and surprises

Ohia in East Maui Watershed watercolor by Katharine Stone Ayers

fog envelopes Ohia forest

Inside

fire crackles

Hail on Deck photo by Katharine Stone Ayers

my dog runs
pants
in hot sun

hailstones
bounce off
red deck

hurricane warning
heavy, dark clouds
lightning flashes

Orange Fish photo by Katharine Stone Ayers

cardinals
pass worms
between them

napped
five times today
no guilt

orange fish
peers at me
behind lily leaf

hey mynah bird
get out
of the road

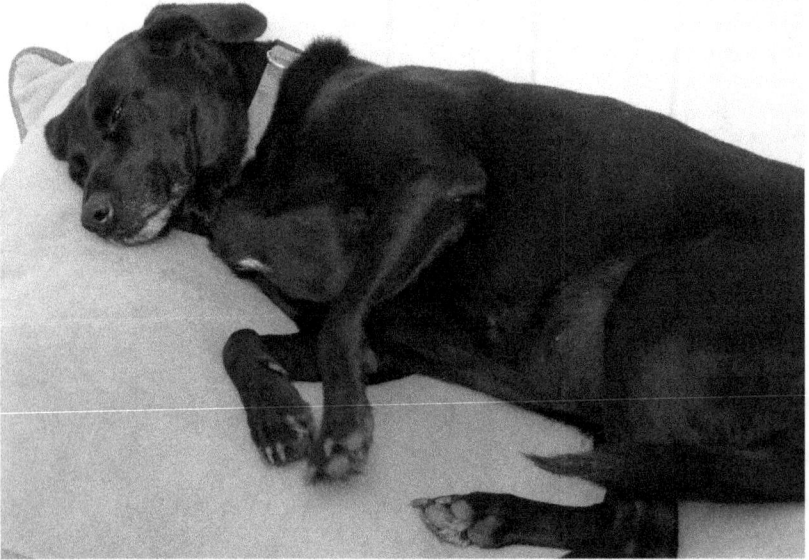
Rosie Snoring photo by Katharine Stone Ayers

Rosie snores

her paws

twitching

Plumeria watercolor painting by Katharine Stone Ayers

moment

of despair

plumerias blooming

LOVE

When I love,
my whole day
gets brighter

PRESENCE DANCES
in the SPACE between US

THE SPACE BETWEEN THEM

A silver haired man
shows a curly haired redhead
which button to push
on a remote control.
Waves of pleasure and bliss
dance between them.

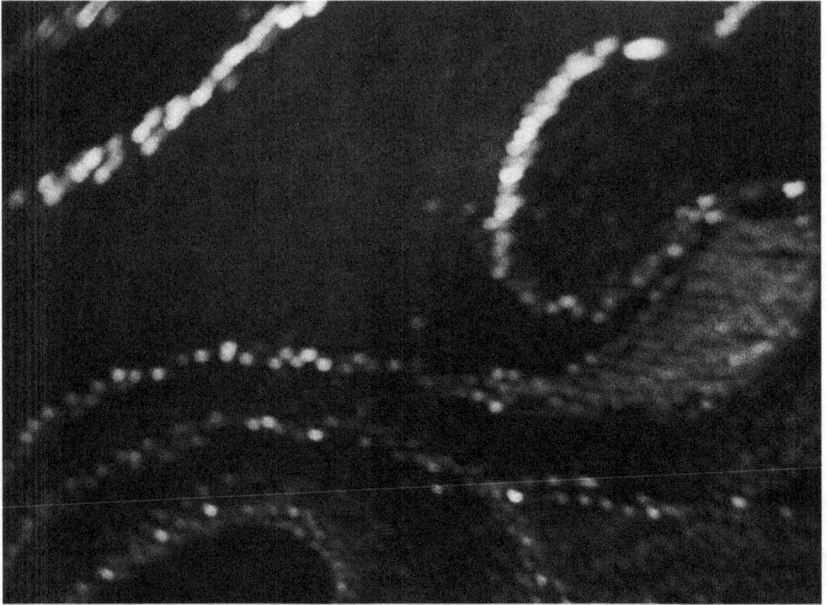

Strands of Gold photo by Katharine Stone Ayers

OUR WORDS like GEMS

A moving Presence
dances
in the space between us.

Strands of gold and black,
love, peace,
red, yellow
joy, sensuality, aliveness
weave us
into a magnificent fabric.

Tensions
in our souls are exposed
by the light of our awareness
and dissolve.

Our words
fall like gems
on each other's bodies,
impact our souls.

A tide takes us
into a realm
of no words.

We fall silent
held in
emptiness.

Georgia

TOUCHED BY GEORGIA

Your words
your deep listening

Silences
touch my heart like a feather
send luminous bubbles
of light rivulets throughout my body

When you stop speaking
luminosity remains
envelops me in delicate rainbow light

Whispered intimacy
Precious connection

Deborah

DEBORAH

We meet today.
Delicate angelic energy
moves through the air like fireflies.

Palpable lightness is present
even though we are talking about cancer,
and "heavy" subjects,
like how to fire people,
set boundaries around abuse,
not accommodate in a way that I am diminished
or overextended financially or energetically.

You ask me what I am writing.
I say I'm writing about trauma,
not for the sake of focusing on trauma,
but for the sake of healing,
becoming whole.

*I want to help people discover that they don't have to be
caught or stuck in their suffering.*

Red and amber pleasure stirs in my genitals and pelvic floor
tickles a large inert stagnant ball in my belly.
Two guardian dogs are growling there.
Protecting a sacred, gentle, fiery, creative delight that rises.

Sweetness between us
brings memories of being with my beloved Grandma
in her rose garden.

Then I had no words to articulate my pain,
but knowing that she loved me deeply
touched my soul,
saved me,
showed me a world of goodness
beyond a world of suffering.

Jonia photo by Katharine Stone Ayers

For JONIA

Kind words
emanating
from your heart.

Compassionate words
put a buffer between me and my history,
place a cushion around my heart,
soften my throat,
relax my shoulders,
touch my soul.

Loving words
bring me home again,
help me to remember who I am,
allow me settle into quiet preciousness.

Queen Protea photo by Katharine Stone Ayers

MY CUP RUNNETH OVER...

remembering the honest words that flowed between us,
how our awareness deepened as we moved into another
reality— gratitude, grace, vast emptiness, circular connection

seeing the last rays of orange gold sun glowing through
grey clouds

hearing the laughter of children frolicking with their
doggies as they run across an expanse of green

feeling the hand of my friend giving Reiki, melting body
tensions, entering a blissful realm deeper than sleep

moving to activate pain in my right hip, as an acupuncturist
twirls needles on the back of my left hand. Magically pain
disappears

listening to my black lab Rosie snore at my feet as light
recedes into a navy velvet sky, wind dies down to a whisper,
birdsong fades

Magnolia photo by Katharine Stone Ayers

HEALING

Today I tried to soothe your suffering,
forgot about your wholeness
looked for a problem
forgot to align
with what is whole in you.

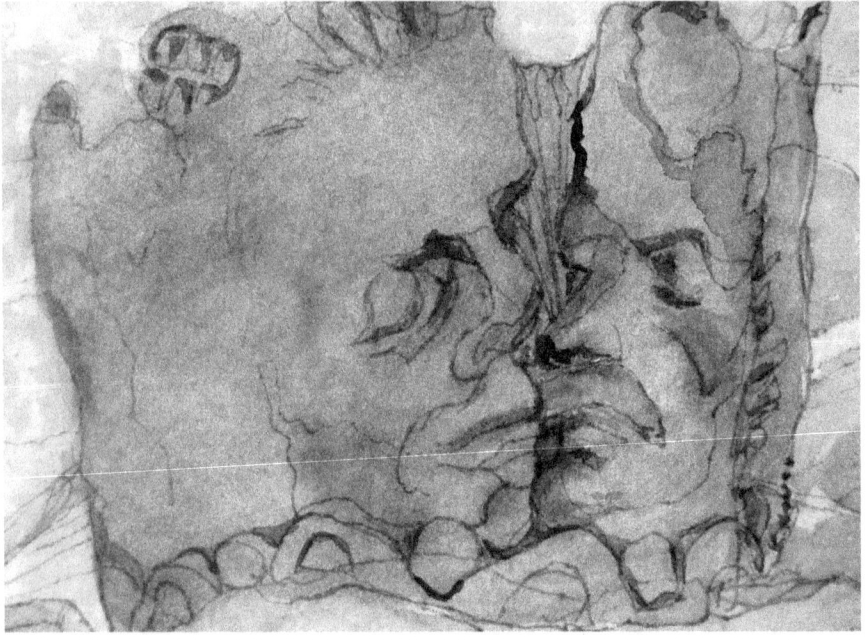

Alchemy watercolor painting by Katharine Stone Ayers

ALCHEMY

Touched
by the alchemy
of our interaction

two sleepy beings
heavy within incessant
inner critic attacks
gradually transform
into scintillating aliveness

lovingly impacted
by the dance of joy
moving through the room.

our little kids let out to play.
Grownups have gone away.

THE CIRCLE IS COMPLETE

A small group of us sit in a living room circle in a *Giving Birth to Yourself* process workshop. From across the circle you ask me, "I want you to tell me that you love me." Your head is bowed down. Your body's collapsed. Your wide eyes look afraid and overwhelmed as if to say, "I'm not sure if am loveable."

My heart bursts with love for you, your openness and transparency. I say, "I love you so much, Charles." You take a deep breath; allow my words to impact you.

I move closer to you, put my hand on your knee. Your foot moves to touch my foot. I place my right foot firmly on your foot. Your body relaxes.

I want you to take in my love. I want the circle of interaction between us to be complete. A simple flow of giving and receiving love.

I'm present with your fear. You let go.

My heart softens. I let love flow. You receive, allow yourself to be nourished. As you take in love, I am healed too.

My whole being is present in the moment. I am totally here with you. You are completely here with me. You are present to yourself. I am present to myself.

The air feels electric. My vision, hearing, sense of touch, taste and smell are heightened. The room looks brighter.

I say "Thank you for letting me love you."

The room fills with Presence. Outside – fushcia bougainvillea, clear blue sky – inside – friends in a circle – everything is luminous, animated and held by love.

In that moment, I know with absolute certainty and clarity that

I am love.
You are love.
We are immersed in an ocean of love.
The circle is complete.

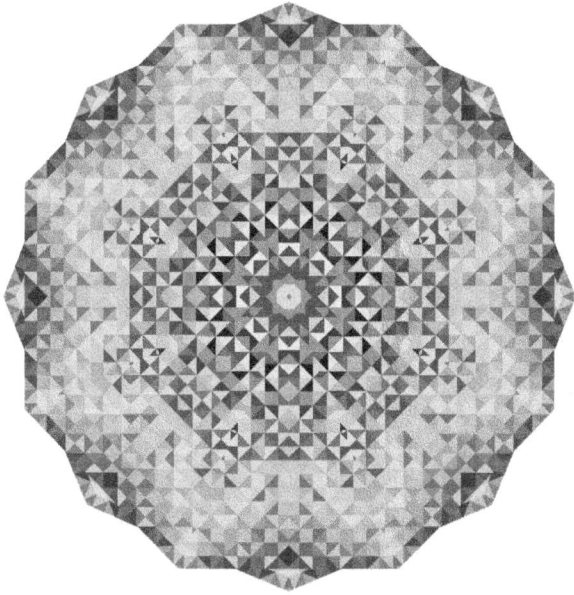

BEAUTY EMERGES

I want connection!
Don't like how familiar friends
fall away, disappear.

I don't want to lose
The predictable way
we've always interacted.

I don't want to be alone!

You say, "Think about it. We die alone.
Being alone is preparation for death."

I say, "I don't want to think about it!"
Too much is disappearing:
people, things I thought I loved,
ways I used to move my body.

I want to keep on doing what I want to do,
what I used to do,
the way I want to do it.

You say,
"What about precious and intimate time
with yourself?"

I say, "It doesn't feel precious, intimate, sacred or anything else!
It's full of busyness, responsibilities, obligations, long to do
lists."

If I take a moment,
to be with myself,
sense, look and listen,

the pull of the external world
loses its glimmer.

beauty emerges from inside:

teeming aliveness,
animated,
kind, gentle, delicate,
diaphanous.

LET LOVE FLOW

O BROTHER SISTER

O brother of capacity and kindness
who runs wildly through the forest
seeking novelty and safe haven
Your heart is willing
but fear restrains you
from melting into the unity of Being

O sister of purity and love
you savor each moment
touch my heart

O Uncle of big heart and many talents
an anchor in any storm
guardian of love, kindness, support
your hands craft beauty

O brother sister of depth and lightheartedness
come play with me

Freesias oil painting by Katharine Stone Ayers

FUN

sleeping under the Milky Way in an Army hammock

lying on the beach watching comets and shooting stars

rolling down the gigantic dunes at Welfleet
getting a belly massage when surfing giant breakers

bicycling to the next town with a best friend
having a sleepover with girlfriends

playing spin the bottle, kissing blonde haired, blue eyed Jimmy

watching multi-colored freesias pop up in random places in my
garden in the beginning of March

arranging red, fuchsia, purple, beige and white blossoms
in my handmade turquoise and lavender vase

sniffing fragrant Cloud roses

smelling jasmine that sprawls around tree stumps and
spreads into the woods in my backyard filling the air with
an intoxicating aroma

seeing my black lab Rosie tuck her head, roll on her back,
snake and swing her spine back and forth to scratch all her
itchy places

enjoying rain pings on the roof in the middle of the night
seeing how rain swirls down in misty gusts catching the early
morning light

going slow and connecting with each moment.
making a collage full of sparkles and glitter
expressing what's alive in me in paint and color
feeling uplifted and held by love

being with a friend, having peppermint tea, onion soup, lamb
curry, speaking passionately from our hearts

sitting down to meditate,
finding places in my Being I call home

Orchid watercolor painting by Katharine Stone Ayers

SILENT LONGING

I know
the silent longing of my heart--
how to be there for you when you tell me you're coming unraveled,
what it feels like to be authentic or phony.

I know
that swimming, dancing, laughing,
breathing deeply,
painting, drawing mindfully, writing poetry makes my heart sing,
the bliss of letting lines flow out of my fingers when drawing
a rose or an orchid.

I know
how much I love your gentle kisses, the way you hold me.

I know
the joy of feeding my mosquito fish when they swim to the surface
and gobble up little pellets,
the satisfaction of being mindful and embracing what arises:
pleasure, pain, sadness, anger, fear, love, joy, bliss.

Sunlight on Fall Leaves photo by Katharine Stone Ayers

MEMORIES THAT HEAL

I remember the scent of pines in the summer air
warm sand under my feet
tree sap sticking to my fingers
squished Wintergreen berries pressed against my nose

Lightning flashes
thunder rocking the walls
winds howling
pines falling across the road
salt water wilting leaves

I remember your gentle kiss
against my cheek
how I melted into you

I remember the excitement of knowing
gentle wisdom guides my life

I remember grandma's smile
how she taught me
we are infused with light

I remember when you told me
you wished you were an octopus
so you could embrace all parts of me

I remember when I was learning how to draw
lotus petals unfolding

I remember when you danced with me
pulled me close
while your friends stomped on the floor
to keep the jukebox playing the same love song
over and over

LET LOVE FLOW

When I look at life
through the lens of my childhood experiences,
reality became distorted, confining, opaque.

Sometimes
I become small,
contract down to the size
of a slug
wallow in lethargy.

When I let love flow
a sparkling yellow love torrent
pours through every cell.

Coral Rose photo by Katharine Stone Ayers

MIRACLES

Who made the smell of the fragrant cloud coral rose,
wind that puffs through shades in my office window,
sways my Arica palms and brings excitement?
Who created Rosie's affection as her nose lifts my arm
begging for a pat,
lies at my feet snoring, follows me around the house?
What brings delight as I splash in the ocean,
currents tickle my belly?
What keeps me loving you?

West Maui Mountains pastel painting by Katharine Stone Ayers

I KNOW

I know the feel of Rosie's cold nose on my skin,
her nudge against my forearm, her silky black ear hairs.

I know how the sun sets over the West Maui mountains
turns the clouds pink, peach and purple.

I know the thrill of cold, fast ocean current against my belly,
the sound of silence, scent of light, color of love.

I know the beauty and holding of Presence.

Goddess photo by Katharine Stone Ayers

IMPERMANENCE

This elegant black beaded dress
will disintegrate one day
But who can rob my heart of joy
or my mind of stillness?

My favorite grandma died
my dog won't live long enough
But who can extinguish my soul's flame
or keep me from singing and dancing?

I abide in the light of the Jasmine Goddess –
no longer hide behind a shell
of performance or pretense.
Without shame – in pure nakedness.

Let Your Trembling Heart Fly print by Katharine Stone Ayers

TREMBLING HEART

Cut
the cords
that tie you
to past
memories,
hopes,
dreams,
lovers

Even though
you may long for
what is gone

Let love flow
Let your trembling heart
fly

www.ingramcontent.com/pod-product-compliance
Lightning Source LLC
LaVergne TN
LVHW021454080426
835509LV00018B/2275